to Elijah

Copyright @2021 Brian K. Fitzpatrick
Web: www.j330life.com   Email: info@j330life.com

Scriptures marked as King James Version are taken from the King James Bible, public domain.

Scripture taken from the New King James Version. Copyright © 1982 by Thomas Nelson, Inc. Used by permission. All rights reserved.

THE HOLY BIBLE, NEW INTERNATIONAL VERSION® NIV®

Copyright © 1973, 1978, 1984 by International Bible Society®

Used by permission. All rights reserved worldwide.

Scripture quotations marked (NLT) are taken from the Holy Bible, New Living Translation, copyright ©1996, 2004, 2015 by Tyndale House Foundation. Used by permission of Tyndale House Publishers, Carol Stream, Illinois 60188. All rights reserved

All Scripture quotations are taken from THE MESSAGE, copyright © 1993, 2002, 2018 by Eugene H. Peterson. Used by permission of NavPress, represented by Tyndale House Publishers. All rights reserved.

Scripture quotations marked (TLB) are taken from The Living Bible copyright © 1971. Used by permission of Tyndale House Publishers, Carol Stream, Illinois 60188. All rights reserved

"Scripture quotations taken from the Amplified® Bible (AMP), Copyright © 2015 by The Lockman Foundation. Used by permission. www.lockman.org"

Library of Congress Control Number (Pending)

Printed in The United States of America

ISBN 978-0-578-89311-2

about THE AUTHOR

BRIAN K. FITZPATRICK
Minister, Life Coach and Leadership Consultant

Brian Fitzpatrick is a native of Columbus, GA, and is a Minister of the Gospel, Life Coach, Leadership Consultant, and Trainer with a passion for helping others reach their full potential through sharing the Word of God and providing Leadership Development opportunities that bring transformation in life and leadership.

Brian has extensive professional leadership experience that focused on organizational operations, community program development, organizational capacity building, leadership development and coaching sales leaders. Brian is the owner of J330Life where he provides business coaching and consulting services to individuals, non-profits, and organizations.

Brian holds several certifications related to the work he is passionate about:

Licensed Minister
Lean Six Sigma Yellow Belt
Certified Life Coach - International Association for Certified Coaches
Certified Right Path Facilitator
Certified Trainer of Servants by Design (Process Communications Model)
Certified Facilitator of Scream Free Parenting

Life Lessons for Achieving Your GOALS one day AT A TIME

contents

GET FOCUSED **6**

RENEW YOUR VISION **8**

ELIMINATE YOUR BLOCKS **20**

SIMPLIFY YOUR ACTIONS **34**

EMBRACE YOUR CHANGES **46**

TARGET YOUR IMPACT **59**

Sometimes in life, we reach points where we have the thought; "man, I sure wish I could press the "reset" button."

the RESET JOURNEY

What we are saying is we wish by some magical something that we can just simply start over. My life is no different.

Full of missed steps, regrets, words that can't be taken back, hurts, trials and triumphs.

At age 6, I remember being awakened by an argument in the middle of the night and my mother, my sister and I left the house walking down the street well after dark going I don't know where. At 8 years old, I remember holding a knife to my chest in my grandmother's kitchen crying and wanting to take my life because I was being bullied.

At the age of 17, I remember walking down the road late at night with my sister and having a gun pulled on me after having words with a stranger passing by who had made a lewd comment to her. But I also remember the coaches, the mentors, the leaders in my life who kept me on the straight and narrow. All those who invested time and resources, gave of themselves to see that me and so many others from the same difficult circumstances did not become a statistic. So here I sit on the verge of finishing my first book I am reflecting on how things truly do come full circle.

Me, the shy kid who you could not have paid to say much now has words not only to say but to share with others. I sit here and realize that through all of the ups and downs there was one thing that I could not put into words then, but I can now. That is that God through every phase, stage, transition in my life never gave up on me. No matter how I missed the mark, how many goals I set and didn't achieve, I could always count on Him to help me "RESET" the table and start again. I don't know what faith you are or where you are in your faith but one thing I want to tell you is that God is the God of the "RESET." When we have lost our way, lost our focus, not walking in our purpose, He is always there to help us get back on course.

This began to manifest in my life in 2013 as I sat at home jobless, pregnant wife (surprise mind you) and feeling helpless and lost. One because as a man, I wondered how I would support a family being jobless and second how could I be a help to a pregnant wife. Mind you this would be the first child for us both. I was afraid, angry, confused and more than anything tired. I wondered "**GOD WHAT ARE YOU DOING**", it was not supposed to be this way, yet it was. I felt helpless.

LIFE WAS HAPPENING BIG TIME!

After seven months, I got a job working helping to develop a program that served the employees of the company. This was a job that I did not apply for by the way. I went in to interview with the CEO for the job I applied for and that interview took a drastic turn as she outlined what she wanted to talk to me about in this other position. It intrigued me but being transparent it was a substantial pay decrease, but I knew God was telling me to do it. Did I mention that by this time my son Elijah, who this book is dedicated to, made his appearance after 26 weeks and 1 day of gestation. He was 1lb 7oz. and 12 inches and the toughest man I have ever met. Like I said life was happening big time! However, in all of this, I realized that when **GOD HAS A PURPOSE** for our lives the picture is always bigger than we ever thought. Over the next three years, I worked alongside many talented people to develop a culture-shifting program for employees where we trained, coached and helped people reach their goals; all while driving each Friday after work to the children's hospital in Atlanta to be with my wife and son. Doctors, treatments, tests, and procedures consumed our lives and my thoughts were getting increasingly hard to sort through and focus. One day while sitting at my son's bedside the word reset kept coming to my mind. I had been praying about a model as a coach that I could use to help clients think through the challenges they faced and develop a plan of action to reach their goals. It was in that moment that God spoke to me and said," **WHAT YOU ARE DOING IS NOT JUST ABOUT THEM IT IS ABOUT YOU ALSO."**

OVER THE NEXT SEVERAL DAYS RESET JUST KEPT COMING BACK TO ME AND FINALLY ONE MORNING GETTING READY FOR WORK, GOD SHOWED ME IT WAS AN ACRONYM:

RENEW YOUR VISION, ELIMINATE YOUR BLOCKS, SIMPLIFY YOUR ACTIONS, EMBRACE CHANGE, TARGET YOUR IMPACT

AS I TYPED THESE WORDS INTO MY PHONE, I KNEW THAT HE WAS SPEAKING TO ME. I AM FIGHTING BACK TEARS AS I TYPE NOW THINKING ABOUT THAT MOMENT.

THIS REVELATION NOT ONLY CHANGED THE WAY I APPROACHED COACHING AND DOING MY 9 TO 5 WORK, BUT IT CHANGED THE WAY THAT I BEGAN TO APPROACH MY OWN LIFE. I HAD ALWAYS BEEN PASSIONATE ABOUT HELPING PEOPLE HAVING WORKED IN THE NON-PROFIT SECTOR AT THIS POINT FOR OVER TWENTY-ONE YEARS. SEEING PEOPLE REACH THEIR GOALS WAS THAT THING THAT SET MY **SOUL ON FIRE**, BUT R.E.S.E.T. TOOK IT MANY STEPS FURTHER BECAUSE I SAW MYSELF IN MY SITUATION APPLYING THESE PRINCIPLES TO MY OWN LIFE.

Fast forward to today, my son passed away two days before the new year in 2015, he would be 7 years old. Being transparent, our marriage did not survive the storm, however, I realized that storms may sometimes get the best of us, that they are only temporary. So, I began my RESET again. I began remembering all of the doors that God opened for me, the opportunities He gave me throughout my life and career and it renewed a fire in me.

Through it all, I have learned to never stop **dreaming**, to never stop **living** and the major part of that is having a vision for our lives.

Setting goals and doing the work to see them come to fruition. We all get 86,400 seconds each day, but the question is what we are going to do with them. Are we going to spend them lamenting what knocked us down or are we going to use them to pick ourselves up and RESET things? I am passionate about this model because it has not only helped me, but I have seen clients get out of debt because that was their goal, shift their business model, and increase their profitability. After all, that was their goal, to become better parents and leaders. In short, we all need to reset at some point. To take a step back, **LOOK AT LIFE AND MAKE A PLAN**. So why not do it the RESET way. This devotional, again, is dedicated to my son Elijah who is with me each day as I walk out my RESET. Because RESET is not a one and done endeavor. It is a mindset shift that transforms the way we take-action. So, you are always doing it. So now nearly 6 years later, I re-engaged in my Leadership Consulting Business J330Life because of him. The name comes from John 3:30 which says, **"HE MUST INCREASE AND I MUST DECREASE."** I am simply a vessel for God to do what He does. Having a child with special needs was the most challenging and rewarding thing I have ever done. As Elijah's father I realized that the greatest contribution we can make is to help pave the way for someone else to reach their full potential. In contrast, the greatest failure we can have is to never have helped anyone. This thought fueled me every day of his life and it is why I do what I do. He **INSPIRED, ENCOURAGED, EMPOWERED** and helped to transform me into the man I am as I write this to you.

SOMETIMES STORMS MAY GET THE BEST OF US, IT IS ONLY *temporary*

I am a witness that **"ALL THINGS WORK TOGETHER FOR GOOD. TO THEM, THAT LOVE GOD AND ARE CALLED ACCORDING TO HIS PURPOSE."**
~ROMANS 8:28

The scriptures contained in this work are here regardless of religion, gender, ethnicity or anything else, to inspire, encourage, empower and transform your mindset on your RESET Journey. In each 10 Day section, there are coaching questions and further instructions to help you paint your RESET picture.

Thank you so much for your support of this endeavor and for allowing me to share a small piece of my story with you before getting to the reading. May God's richest blessings be upon you and your families.

Be blessed and encouraged

GET FOCUSED

Before we dive in, I need to share with you one key element to the entire process. This would be the lead in question that your work in using The RESET Model will be based on. You must first always answer the question, "WHAT AM I FOCUSING ON?"

This is important because:

It gives focus to your thought process so that you can use the model most efficiently.

It is easy to get bogged down in a hundred different things going through our minds at once. I call this chasing "squirrels."

After you have completed the process, phase two is building your action plan. Once you know what problem you are working on, the action planning process is that much easier.

Examine where you are right now and answer the following questions.

What are my 3 biggest priorities at this moment?

What is the MOST important thing I want to complete right now?

Is this still important enough for you to go through the RESET Model?

What could you do to make sure that this is a goal you can commit to?

Do not conform to the pattern of this world, but **BE TRANSFORMED** BY THE RENEWING of your mind. Romans 12:2

RENEW YOUR VISION

Simply put, vision is the outward expression of inward images we have around our goals.

A vision must be written down.

"It's not what you look at that matters, it is what you see!"

-Henry David Thoreau

Writing down our vision creates commitment, accountability, and structure to what you say you want. When it comes to going after our goals, you may find yourself in that place I call "stuck." You probably are familiar with it because it can be identified by the fact that you have lost the motivation to pursue the very thing that you said you wanted.

Therefore RENEWING OUR VISION is step one in The RESET Model.

This will serve as the foundation on which you build everything else.

DAY 1

2 Corinthians 5:17

"Therefore, if anyone is in Christ, he is a new creation. The old has passed away; behold, the new has come."

At various points in our lives, we will go through renewal processes. It's like a computer that is upgraded regularly. Because of the needs of the environment, changes, solutions, patches, and upgrades need to be applied to keep it functioning at the optimal level. This all comes through a renewed vision of who we are, who we want to be and where we desire to go. When we align with God's will for our lives, we receive this renewal on the inside through salvation ("that if you confess with your mouth the Lord Jesus and believe in your heart that God raised Him from the grave, you will be saved." Romans 10:9).

The Holy Spirit gives new life to our character and to our heart for the things of God's heart. We are not reformed or rehabilitated, but we are new creations. As a new creation, we are now positioned to begin to *Renew the Vision* for our life, our goals, our families, our work and our purpose. You are made new.

TODAY'S ASSIGNMENT

MAKE A LIST OF AREAS OF YOUR LIFE WHERE YOU NEED TO RENEW YOUR VISION. WHAT SPECIFICALLY DO YOU WANT TO SEE HAPPEN IN THOSE AREAS?

_____

_____

_____

_____

_____

_____

_____

DAY 2

Psalm 51:10
"Create in me a clean heart, O God, and renew a right spirit within me."

2006 was one of the darkest times in my life. I remember sitting on the living room floor of a now- empty apartment and thinking that God had forgotten about me. If I can be transparent, I lived a life at this time that was far less than what God desired, and I knew it. I had drifted far from the things that I had been taught, and I was living life on my terms. As I sat, God reminded me that even when we get off course, we need only to ask Him to make us clean from within and fill us with new thoughts and desires. The first step in *Renewing our Vision* for our lives is renewing our connection with the Father. Right conduct, actions, and guided vision can only come from a clean heart and right spirit.

TODAY'S ASSIGNMENT

WHAT DOES HAVING A CLEAN HEART AND RIGHT SPIRIT MEAN TO YOU? HOW CAN THIS HELP YOU TO RENEW YOUR VISION?

_____
_____
_____
_____
_____
_____
_____

DAY 3

Romans 12:2
"Do not conform to the pattern of this world but be transformed by the renewing of your mind."

We live in a world that is full of duplicates. We see car companies making their version of the same vehicle; we hear music, though, from different artists, it has the same sound and most definitely people who live their lives based on trying to fit into what "the norm" is. The Apostle Paul tells the people not to be conformed to what you see in the world. In other words, don't duplicate their customs and practices. Don't try to fit in, but rather, allow God to transform the way you think and see. When we allow God to renew our minds, transform the way we think and see, we are setting ourselves up to see God move in ways that we have never experienced.

TODAY'S ASSIGNMENT

WHAT DOES HAVING A RENEWED MIND MEAN TO YOU? HOW IS YOUR MINDSET KEEPING YOU FROM WHERE YOU WANT TO GO IN THE AREAS YOU IDENTIFIED ON DAY 1?

_____
_____
_____
_____
_____
_____
_____

DAY 4

Isaiah 40:31
"But they who wait for the Lord shall renew their strength; they shall mount up with wings like eagles; they shall run and not be weary; they shall walk and not faint."

Patience is one area in my life where I know my mind has been renewed. I was the guy that touted not being "the most patient person in the world." As a leader of people, I realized that it put others on edge with me, and it hindered communication because they thought that I would fly off the handle. One of my mentors who spent 35 years in the military sat me down one day, looked me square in the eyes and told me "stop." He then explained to me how being impatient gave access to all these other things like anger, resentment, and jealousy of others. If I did not want to be that guy also, then I needed to "stop."

This verse tells us that if we can just wait and be patient, our strength to endure will be renewed. Often, we don't see our goals come to fruition because the process seems so long, and we want it right now, so we determine that we will just quit. When we learn to wait on God, we condition our minds to not focus on the now but to keep our eyes on what is to come, where we are going. Strength comes through the process of patience.

TODAY'S ASSIGNMENT
HOW HAS THE PROCESS OF PATIENCE BEEN DEVELOPED IN YOUR LIFE?

_____

_____

_____

_____

_____

_____

_____

DAY 5

Ephesians 4:23

"Instead, let the Spirit renew your thoughts and attitudes…"

One of the biggest hindrances in lives can be our attachment to the past. How we "used to be," "used to think" or "used to do it." In the corporate world, the growth of companies can come to a screeching halt if they are stuck in the place of "use to." They must continue to drive forward to the new and that can only come by taking lessons from the past but not bringing the past with them. So, it is also with us individually, we must make a conscious decision to leave that place of "use to" and allow God to renew our thoughts and attitudes. Our thoughts and attitudes not only about the world around us or our goals but about ourselves. We must begin to see ourselves as God sees us, "fearfully and wonderfully made" (Psalm 139:14)

TODAY'S ASSIGNMENT

HOW ARE YOUR THOUGHTS AND ATTITUDES ABOUT YOURSELF HELPING OR HINDERING YOU? HAVE YOU ALLOWED GOD TO RENEW YOUR MIND? WHY OR WHY NOT?

_____
_____
_____
_____
_____
_____
_____

DAY 6

2 Timothy 1:6
"For this reason, I remind you to fan into flame the gift of God, which is in you through the laying on of my hands."

When I was in Boy Scouts as a kid, I remember how much I loved it when we went camping. My favorite part was always starting the fire but also learning how to keep it going. You didn't always have to add new wood, but most of the time, all you had to do was fan it and blow on it a little for the fire to rekindle. I now realize that what we were doing by blowing away the old ash and removing objects that were smothering the fire, was allowing new oxygen to fuel and reignite the flame.

We can find ourselves in a place where we are not as excited about what we are doing as maybe we once were. Maybe we are not as excited about our job, marriage, calling, ministry or even chasing our dreams. In those times, through our actions, we must begin to fan away the things that have built up and are trying to smother the flame. Then through the Word of God, begin to breathe (2 Timothy 3:16-17) new oxygen into the atmosphere to fuel and reignite the flame. You have a say in the combustion process. Remove the old and introduce something new.

TODAY'S ASSIGNMENT

WHAT GIFTS AND TALENTS DO YOU HAVE THAT YOU ARE NOT REALLY USING TO HELP REACH YOUR GOALS AND WHY?

_____
_____
_____
_____
_____
_____
_____

DAY 7

Jeremiah 29:11

"For I know the plans I have for you, declares the Lord, plans for good and not for evil, to give you a future and a hope."

We've all had people in our lives; leaders, teachers, parents, coaches, pastors, friends that have encouraged us along the way to keep going even when things were tough. God orchestrates those encounters in our life because that is His nature as a leader. He knows how He created us and what He has placed in us, so there is never a doubt for Him that we can do everything single thing that He has for us to do. Things may not always go as planned, but as long as we have God on our side, who knows the future and the plans that He has for us, we can be confident that the conclusion of the matter will be in our favor to live the "Zoe" life. The God kind of life.

TODAY'S ASSIGNMENT

WHAT CAN YOU START DOING TODAY TO HEP ALIGN YOURSLEF WITH GOD'S PLAN FOR YOUR LIFE?

_____
_____
_____
_____
_____
_____
_____

DAY 8

Galatians 5:22-23
"But the fruit of the Spirit is love, joy, peace, patience, kindness, goodness, faithfulness, gentleness, self-control; against such things, there is no law."

Our mental attitude in going after the vision we see for our life is crucially important. If we do not keep the proper perspective, we can become puffed up in pride, thinking we did it all by ourselves. Here we find some key ingredients that we need to cultivate in our character to help keep us from allowing our accomplishments to become idols in our lives. We should love what we do, do it with joy, be at peace when there are setbacks, have patience during the process, show kindness to those in our path, exhibit goodness through excellence, show faithfulness to what God has placed in us to do, speak with gentleness, walk-in self-control and we will be well on our way to Christ-centered achievement.

TODAYS' ASSIGNMENT

GIVE EXAMPLES OF THE HOW YOU SEE THE FRUIT OF THE SPIRIT IN YOUR LIFE.

_____
_____
_____
_____
_____
_____
_____

DAY 9

Hosea 6:3

"Oh, that we might know the Lord! Let us press on to know Him. He will respond to us as surely as the arrival of dawn or the coming of rains in early spring."

Before we can know our purpose, which directly connects to the vision for your life, we must first know God. The Bible says in John 17:3, "And this is life eternal, that they may know You, the only true God, and Jesus Christ whom You have sent." In other words, knowing God is the most important thing we can do and the sum of everything that we do or dream. Seek first to know Him and all the things will be added to you. (Matthew 6:33)

TODAY'S ASSIGNMENT

WHAT CAN YOU BEGIN DOING TO GET KNOW GOD OR KNOW HIM BETTER?

___

___

___

___

___

___

DAY 10

Galatians 6:9
"And let us not grow weary of doing good, for in due season we will reap, if we do not give up.

I was surprised to find out recently that kids still played hide and seek. This was a staple when I was growing up, but there was one problem: there was always this one kid that hid well, and no one could find them. I wonder if anyone reading this was that kid… At any rate, if you were the seeker this was extremely frustrating. I must admit there were times where I just gave up the search. I did not win the game because I got tired and quit. Sometimes life can happen so much that we just want to quit. If that is you, be encouraged and know that if you just stay consistent and focused on doing the right things that you will, in the end, reap a harvest of blessings because of the good you sowed into your own life and the lives of others.

TODAY'S ASSIGNMENT

WHAT SEEDS OF DOING GOOD HAVE YOU SOWN IN THE LAST 7 DAYS?

___

___

___

___

___

___

RENEW YOUR VISION | **REFLECTION**

STEP ONE TO RENEWING YOUR VISION IS ALLOWING GOD TO RENEW YOUR MIND AND REFOCUS YOUR PURPOSE. STEP TWO IS WRITING THE VISION. HERE IS WHERE YOU BEGIN TO WRITE THE VISION!

What is it that you want? What is your goal?

Who are you now, and who will you need to become to complete your goal?

What would you be able to do if there were not obstacles?

Imagine for a moment that you have made it to your goal. How did you get there?

_____
_____
_____
_____
_____
_____
_____
_____
_____
_____

Habakkuk 2:2 ~The Lord answered me and said: "Write the vision and make it plain on tablets, That he may run who reads it."

ELIMINATE YOUR BLOCKS

WHAT ARE **BLOCKS**?

Let's say you are driving down the road and there is construction happening. In some cases, the road is impassable so there are barriers put out that keep drivers from going past a certain point. Hence the name "roadblock." Our mental blocks around goals work the same way. They are barriers that keep us from getting to our destinations.

No matter which block we are dealing with, we must identify them, assess them for validity and then move towards solving them so that they no longer hinder our progress. Our achievement of any goal in life is contingent upon being able to identify when something has moved from simply being an obstacle to an actual block. Once we do that, we can then formulate a very specific plan to work through the blocks and get moving again.

> "TO ACHIEVE YOUR GOALS, YOU HAVE TO
>
> *Eliminate*
>
> YOUR OBJECTIONS TO THE GOAL,
> NOT ARGUE THE OBJECTIONS."
>
> Brian K. Fitzpatrick

QUESTIONS I NEED TO ANSWER ABOUT REACHING MY GOAL

Where do you think your thoughts could be getting in the way?
_____
_____
_____

What does your block tell you?
_____
_____
_____

What areas of your life do you need to not be so hard on yourself? (Make a list)
_____
_____
_____

Why are you so hard on yourself in those ares and how are you going to improve?
_____
_____
_____

DAY 11

2 Corinthians 10:5

"We destroy arguments and every lofty opinion raised against the knowledge of God and take every thought captive to obey Christ."

Some of the biggest arguments I have had in my life have been with myself in my mind. I know what it is that I want, but yet there is all this back and forth, talking myself into and then out of acting. One of the greatest battles that we will ever fight in our lives is in our minds. That is where the enemy tries to come in and do his work to discourage us, make us fearful and make us think that God is not true to His word for our lives. As Spirit-empowered believers we must grab hold of and eliminate every one of those self-defeating thoughts by releasing it to God. 1 Peter 5:7 says "cast all your anxiety on Him because He cares for you." I know letting go can be difficult but if we don't, these thoughts can become the very things that keep us from getting "there."

TODAY'S ASSIGNMENT

WHAT CONCERNS OR FEARS DO YOU HAVE ABOUT GOING AFTER YOUR GOAL? WHAT PART OF THAT DO YOU NEED TO GIVE TO GOD?

DAY 12

Romans 8:28
"And we know that God causes everything to work together for the good of those who love God and are called according to His purpose for them."

Growing up in tough neighborhoods and housing projects, I know what it is to not have a lot. Many times, we depended on our mom to bring home food from the restaurants at which she worked at night. This was our only meal from home because breakfast and lunch were free at school. Even at a young age, I dreamed of things getting better because my mom always would tell us "it won't always be this way." I don't know where her faith was at the time, but I know now that all things truly do work together for the good. The key though, is to love God and be called (saved) according to His purpose. Tests, trials and hard times do not define us, but they refine us because God takes those things and uses them to make us into the men and women He has called us to be. Our part, however, is to not allow those things to keep us from moving forward. Remember, all things work together for the good.

TODAY'S ASSIGNMENT

WHAT ARE THE TIMES FROM YOUR LIFE THAT YOU BELIEVE HELPED YOU GROW THE MOST? HOW DID THEY HELP YOU CHANGE?

_____
_____
_____
_____
_____
_____
_____

DAY 13

2 Corinthians 12:9

"Each time he said, my grace is all you need. My power works best in weakness."

If we read back just a few verses, we will find that Paul was given a thorn in his flesh to keep him from becoming proud because of all the mighty things he had done in the name of the Lord. Paul had something in his life that was there for the express purpose of keeping him from falling into a mindset of "self". We will have things that come against us that seemingly block our path to progress even if we are doing the right things. Although God did not remove Paul's thorn, He did promise to demonstrate His power in Paul's life by letting him know that His grace was enough, or in other words, all he needed. As we recognize more clearly our limitations, we will better recognize our need for God in our lives.

TODAY'S ASSIGNMENT

WHAT IS ONE STRUGGLE THAT YOU DEAL WITH BUT YOU KNOW THAT GOD IS ALWAYS IN IT WITH YOU?

_____

_____

_____

_____

_____

_____

DAY 14

Romans 16:17

"And now I make one more appeal, my dear brothers and sisters. Watch out for people who cause divisions and upset people's faith by teaching things contrary to what you have been taught. Stay away from them."

Throughout my life as a leader, minister, and coach, I have come to understand that we all have blocks. We can look at blocks as bad habits or mindsets that obstruct our will to move forward. However, it is important to understand that people can also be blocks. Blocks are what keep us from pursuing a goal or path. We must assess our circle to ensure that we have people who are in alignment and in support of our aspirations, beliefs, and faith. Be mindful of the circle.

TODAY'S ASSIGNMENT

WHO ARE THE PEOPLE IN YOUR SUPPORT CIRCLE?

_____

_____

_____

_____

_____

_____

_____

DAY 15

Romans 5:3

"We can rejoice, too, when we run into problems and trials, for we know that they help us develop endurance."

In our life journey, we are becoming and overcoming, often at the same time. The problems and setbacks we run into serve to help build our perseverance muscle, which turns into character muscles, which deepen our trust in God and give us confidence about our future. To get stronger, we must build muscle and to build muscle we must lift heavy.

TODAY'S ASSIGNMENT

TALK ABOUT A TIME IN YOUR LIFE THAT HELPED BUILD YOUR ENDURANCE.

_____

_____

_____

_____

_____

_____

_____

DAY 16

Isaiah 57:14

"God says, 'Rebuild the road! Clear away the rocks and stones so my people can return from captivity.'"

In construction, before the structure can be erected, the ground that it is to be built upon must be cleared. Dirt must be moved, trees cut down, rocks and other debris discarded, and the ground made level. As we build upon our dreams and visions, we must do some ground-clearing and leveling. We must ensure we have the right foundation to build something that will withstand the test of time. Level ground makes for the best building conditions.

TODAY'S ASSIGNMENT

WHAT ARE THREE THINGS THAT YOU CAN DO TODAY TO HELP PUT YOU ON THE PATH TO YOUR GOALS?

_____
_____
_____
_____
_____
_____
_____

DAY 17

Psalms 127:1
"Unless the Lord builds a house the work of the builders is wasted."

Have you ever met people who are always drawn to the next big thing? They live their lives for the new fads and trends. This type of lifestyle is unstable and can lead to being unreliable. We need stability if we are going to be in it for the long haul. We cannot be shaken by obstacles or the things of the world. God is the master architect and builder. Trust Him to draw the plan, to give you the vision and equip you to go and build it.

TODAY'S ASSIGNMENT

WHO ARE THE PEOPLE THAT HAVE INFLUENCED YOUR MINDSET, FOR THE GOOD IN YOU LIFE? HOW ARE YOU ALLOWING GOD TO BE ARCHITECT AND BUILDER IN YOUR LIFE?

_____
_____
_____
_____
_____
_____

DAY 18

Philippians 4:6-7

"Don't worry about anything; instead, pray about everything. Tell God what you need and thank Him for all He has done. Then you will experience God's peace, which exceeds anything we can understand. His peace will guard your hearts and minds as you live in Christ Jesus."

Having peace in our lives is a choice that we must make, and we must take action daily to ensure that peace. True peace is not found in simply thinking positively, in the absence of conflict or opposition or even by "feeling good." It comes from knowing that God is in control no matter the circumstances. Stop worrying, pray, tell God what you need, thank Him in advance and watch Him do it.

TODAY'S ASSIGNMENT

HAVE YOU EVER HAD THIS TYPE OF PEACE? WHAT WAS GOING ON WHEN YOU EXPERIENCED THIS? IF YOU HAVEN'T, WOULD YOU LIKE TO?

_____
_____
_____
_____
_____
_____
_____

DAY 19

2 Corinthians 6:3
"We put no obstacle in anyone's way, so that no fault may be found with our ministry."

In everything he did, Paul always considered what his actions conveyed about Jesus. While we do want to eliminate blocks that hinder our progress, let us not become a block because of careless, unthoughtful, and undisciplined actions on our part. Just as Paul did not want to be the excuse for anyone to reject Christ, we should make sure we are encouraging those who are watching that may not be as far along as we are, and not discouraging.

TODAY'S ASSIGNMENT

HOW DO YOU PLAY THE ROLE OF ENCOURAGER FOR THOSE CLOSEST TO YOU?

_____

_____

_____

_____

_____

_____

_____

DAY 20

Hebrews 10:35
"Therefore do not throw away your confidence, which has a great reward."

The Bible gives us two clear directions for life because life often has a fork in the road. If we are to be successful, we must take the higher road. That road is steep, full of obstacles, sometimes slippery but there is a peak just ahead. When on the road to success, we don't throw away our confidence because we don't know where the road leads. You will pass many exits but know that they are not for you. You have somewhere to go.

TODAY'S ASSIGNMENT

HOW WOULD YOU DESCRIBE THE SCENERY ON YOUR ROAD TO SUCCESS THUS FAR? WHAT HAVE BEEN A FEW THINGS THAT HAVE HINDERED YOU?

_____
_____
_____
_____
_____
_____
_____

ELIMINATE YOUR BLOCKS | **REFLECTION**

Imagine for a moment you have achieved your goal(s), how did you get there? (Begin from the end)

What are you ready to change? What are you not ready to change?

What haven't you admitted out loud yet?

What is the issue in a nutshell? What is it in one sentence? What is it in one word?

How important is this to you?

What is the easy way forward (Simplest first step)?

Think of someone you admire. What would they do in this situation?

GOALS WITHOUT DUE DATES ARE SIMPLY *wishes*

SIMPLIFY YOUR ACTIONS

In a world where we are driven by the desire to be better than the next person and fueled by our need to "impress," we find ourselves often making things way more complicated than need be. When it comes to the actions around our goals, it is not about quantity but quality. It is not about how many things we do; it is about doing the right things.

"Simplicity is the ultimate sophistication"
– Leonardo da Vinci

These are actions that create true movement in our life around our goals. Now that we have worked our way through what I call the "clarity steps" (Renew Your Vision and Eliminate Your Blocks), now it is time to begin to put some hands and feet to those goals and get moving. The ability to achieve anything in life is directly connected to the actions we take or do not take. Goals without due dates are simply wishes, so when we begin to think about how to simplify our actions, we are forced on finding our internal motivations to drive external actions.

"Everyone has complicated lives, but the more you can
SIMPLIFY IT
and make it work for you; the better it is going to be.
-Lewis Hamilton

DAY 21

Psalm 116:6
"The Lord preserves the simple; when I was brought low, he saved me."

When I think of simplicity, I think of kids. The way they view things is through the lens of what Jesus described as "childlike faith." Faith to trust that their parents will love them again after being upset because of something they did wrong, faith to know they will have clothes to wear and food to eat. Simply put, they just believe! When we look at keeping it simple from this point of view, we learn that somewhere along the line, between childhood and adulthood, we tend to lose this perspective. As adults, we do a great job of making things way more complicated than necessary. Keeping our actions simple does not mean we are putting out less effort, it just means that we are getting right to the things that matter most and executing upon them. Keep it simple!

TODAY'S ASSIGNMENT

WHERE IN YOUR LIFE CAN YOU STAND A LITTLE MORE SIMPLICITY?

_____
_____
_____
_____
_____
_____
_____

DAY 22

1 John 2:6
"Those who say they live in God should live their lives as Jesus did."

To walk as Christ did for us means living out the example, He set for us. Jesus had a powerful ministry, but if you think about it, He lived a simple life. True, He did not have the technological things that we have, but He kept it simple. He called simple, ordinary people that He would teach, train and send out to do extraordinary things. He did not have e-learning options, fancy presentations or manuals from which to train them. He used actions, example, and spoken wisdom: a simple system that made a great impact. We should all take note of this and remember that less is more and simple still works.

TODAY'S ASSIGNMENT

THINK OF SOMEONE YOU ADMIRE AND ASK THEM HOW THEY KEEP SOMETHING THEY DO SIMPLE?

_____
_____
_____
_____
_____
_____
_____

DAY 23

Proverbs 21:5
"The plans of the diligent lead to profit as surely as haste leads to poverty."

I remember seeing a documentary on Michael Jordan some years ago, and in the piece, they talked about how, at one time, he did not make his high school basketball team. What was more interesting to me, however, was what happened after that. He began to talk about all the hours and hours of practice he put in alone just shooting the ball. I was amazed to see that type of work ethic from someone so young. The following season he made the team, and the rest is history. Diligence is required in being good at anything we do but especially when we have tried and failed. The text says that "the plans" with an S, lead to profit. So, in other words, truly diligent people are solution-driven. They know that sometimes plans must be scaled down or ramped up, but either way, it will lead them where they want to go.

TODAY'S ASSIGNMENT

WHAT IS YOUR MICHAEL JORDAN STORY? TALK ABOUT A TIME WHERE YOU HAD TO GO BACK TO THE DRAWING BOARD?

_____
_____
_____
_____
_____
_____

DAY 24

Proverbs 6:6
"Take a lesson from the ants, you lazy bones. Learn from their ways and become wise."

Ants, to the natural eye, are small, unimposing, and to some, insignificant. Guess it's a good thing that they don't see themselves that way. Daily, they work together, moving about in their simple, straight lines until they get the job done. I wonder what would happen if we took to heart what Archimedes said like the ants do, "The shortest distance between two points is a straight line."

TODAY'S ASSIGNMENT

IF YOU COULD SHORTEN THE TIME IT TAKES TO DO ONE THING IN YOUR LIFE WHAT WOULD IT BE?

_____
_____
_____
_____
_____
_____
_____

DAY 25

1 Corinthians 6:12

"All things are lawful for me, but not all things are helpful. All things are lawful for me, but I will not be enslaved by anything."

There is an old saying "Just because you can does not mean you should." In other words, we have the freedom to make decisions that on the surface, could benefit us in some way. But often, that is simply a disguise that masks the underlying consequences it could have for us or even someone else. We must be careful that what we desire to achieve does not become an obsession that controls us, causes us to fall into pride or even causes harm to someone else. That is not God's will.

TODAY'S ASSIGNMENT

TALK ABOUT A TIME WHERE YOU LEARNED A LIFE LESSON BECAUSE OF AN ACTION YOU TOOK.

_____
_____
_____
_____
_____
_____
_____

DAY 26

2 Corinthians 5:20

"Therefore, we are ambassadors for Christ, God making His appeal through us. We implore you on behalf of Christ, be reconciled to God."

An ambassador is an official representative of one country to another. We are each ambassadors of Christ to the world. Our life and our actions tell a story. We must make sure we take full advantage of the opportunity to make an impact through how we live and what we do. The world is watching.

TODAY'S ASSIGNMENT

WHAT IS SOMETHING SIMPLE YOU CAN DO TO BE AN AMBASSADOR FOR CHRIST?

DAY 27

Ephesians 2:10

"For we are God's handiwork, created in Christ Jesus to do good works, which God prepared in advance for us to do."

Simply put, each of us being God's handiwork was with a simple focus: "to do good works, which God prepared in advance for us to do." So, before we are even "ready," we are on God's mind. Hear the Word of the Lord; "In our simple mandate we are designed to have an extraordinary impact." This is the true benefit of keeping things simple. Receive it!

TODAY'S ASSIGNMENT

THINKING ABOUT THIS TEXT, WHAT DOES IT MEAN TO YOU? WHAT IS GOD SAYING TO YOU?

_____
_____
_____
_____
_____
_____
_____

DAY 28

Exodus 14:15

"And the LORD said to Moses, 'Why do you cry to Me? Tell the children of Israel to go forward."

Here, the Lord tells Moses to stop praying and get on with it. Now make no mistake, prayer is a vital part of everything that we strive to accomplish. However, if we are honest with ourselves, we know what to do, but we continue to pray for "signs," "guidance," "vision," "a word" or "confirmation" as an excuse to not get on with it or even to try and get out of doing it completely. So, simply put, if you know what you are to do, then it is time to get moving.

TODAY'S ASSIGNMENT

IS THERE SOMETHING THAT YOU ARE PRAYING ABOUT CONCERNING YOUR GOAL(S) AND THERE IS A SIMPLE FIRST STEP YOU HAVE NOT TAKEN?

_____

_____

_____

_____

_____

_____

_____

DAY 29

Proverbs 22:29
"Sees thou a man diligent in his business? He shall stand before kings; he shall not stand before mean men."

When you commit yourself to being about the business at hand, you will be surprised where it leads you. Diligence is a quality that is hard to quantify, but it is easy to spot. It is not winning the most awards or even being the first to do it. What it is though is an indispensable part of your plan to bring your dreams into reality.

TODAY'S ASSIGNMENT

WRITE DOWN SOMETHING THAT YOU WANT GOD TO DO THAT IS SO BIG, IT WILL HAVE TO BE HIM TO DO IT.

_____

_____

_____

_____

_____

_____

_____

DAY 30

Colossians 3:23
"Whatever you do, work at it with all your heart, as working for the Lord, not for men."

It makes our work holy when we do it with our hearts as if we are doing it for the Lord. It is one of the greatest honors we can have in taking our gifts and talents and applying them, not only in ministry settings but in the marketplace as well. Let's be honest, there are far more people in the marketplace than are in church on Sunday. So, working this way is a prime opportunity to put our best foot forward, be excellent in what we do, wherever we may do it, therefore, bringing glory to God.

TODAY'S ASSIGNMENT

WHAT IS A SIMPLE THING YOU CAN DO TODAY TO USE YOUR GIFTS RIGHT WHERE YOU ARE?

SIMPLIFY YOUR ACTIONS | **REFLECTION**

What would it take for you to MAKE this happen?

What unproductive actions are you willing to give up for actions that get results?

How could you break this down into smaller, more manageable steps?

Tell me how you will feel once you have completed your actions?

_____
_____
_____
_____
_____
_____
_____
_____
_____
_____
_____
_____

How will you reward yourself when complete?

EMBRACE YOUR CHANGES

The Greek Philosopher Heraclitus said that "the only constant in life is change."

Given just the technological advances we have seen throughout history, I think we can all agree that he was right. So, why then is change so difficult for many of us? In my experience, I have found that difficulty in dealing with change usually comes down to two things: fear and comfort.

When we truly begin to embrace our changes, we will see all the possibilities in what we want to accomplish. When we do that, we get an excitement on the inside that put both fear and comfort in their proper place.

" OUR LIFE DOES NOT GET BETTER CHANCE. IT GET'S BETTER BY **CHANGE**

embrace

Jim Rohn

DAY 31

Isaiah 41:13

"For I am the Lord your God who takes hold of your right hand and says to you. Do not fear; I will help you."

When it comes to making changes in our lives, there are several reasons we don't embrace it fully and more immediately. At the top of the list, you will find fear. Fear can be a very imposing foe. It can keep us tied to past failures, past mistakes and keep us second-guessing. God promises that He will hold our hand as we walk, and most importantly, tells us there is nothing to be afraid of because He will help us, to it and, through it. The question is will we reach and grab His extended hand?

TODAY'S ASSIGNMENT

TALK ABOUT A TIME WHERE GOD HELD YOUR HAND THROUGH A STORM IN YOUR LIFE.

DAY 32

Malachi 3:6

"For I am the Lord, I do not change; Therefore, you are not consumed, O sons of Jacob."

The conclusion of the Book of Malachi brings us to 400 years of silence by God. In the 400 years between Malachi, the last book in the Old Testament, and Matthew, the first book in the New Testament, there were no prophets raised and no messages sent to the people. This was God's final say before Jesus enters the scene. I love this book because in it, God reminds us that He does not change, and because of that, we are not consumed.

He does not change, so we are free to change and be made alive through Christ Jesus. Whether spiritually, emotionally, physically or mentally, change in our lives is the catalyst for growth. If you want to achieve your goals, you must be willing to change.

TODAY'S ASSIGNMENT

MAKE A LIST OF THREE CHANGES YOU KNOW YOU NEED TO MAKE BUT HAVEN'T. HOW ARE THESE THINGS KEEPING YOU FROM REACHING YOUR GOAL(S)?

_____
_____
_____
_____
_____
_____
_____

DAY 33

Deuteronomy 31:6
"So be strong and courageous! Do not be afraid and do not panic before them. For the Lord your God will personally go ahead of you. He will neither fail you nor abandon you."

I remember being 10 years old and standing in my grandmother's kitchen crying because I was being picked on at school because of my weight. I could not understand how people could be so mean, and I remember saying to her that I was never going to school again. Well, you can imagine how that went. Yes, I was sent back day after day, year after year still struggling with my weight, but her words were that God was always with me, and I could talk to Him whenever I wanted. That was hard to understand as a 10-year-old, but I must tell you that when I look back, what she was telling me was to be strong and courageous. Over the years, the schools changed, and the people changed, but God never did. During our seasons of difficulty and change trust in the fact that God is there with you so be strong and courageous.

TODAY'S ASSIGNMENT

TALK ABOUT A TIME WHEN YOU HAD TO BE STRONG AND COURAGEOUS.

_____
_____
_____
_____
_____
_____
_____

DAY 34

Ecclesiastes 3:1
"For everything, there is a season, a time for every activity under Heaven."

Simply put, we have all said that we don't have time for this or that, but we manage to get done the things that are most important to us. Therefore, time is not an issue. The real issue is us not wanting to change our routine. Whether it is prayer, reading the word, going to church, getting to work on time, spending time with your spouse-- if it is important enough to us, we must be willing to change up those routines, rearrange those priorities and make it happen. We all get 86,400 seconds in our day, but what we do with them is up to us.

TODAY'S ASSIGNMENT

HOW CAN YOU ADJUST YOUR SCHEDULE TO MAKE MORE TIME FOR THE THINGS THAT ARE MOST IMPORTANT TO YOU?

_____

_____

_____

_____

_____

_____

_____

DAY 35

Hebrews 6:19
"We have this hope as an anchor for our soul, firm and secure."

A curtain once hung between the Holy Place and the Highest Place in the temple of the Lord. The priest could only enter once each year to make an atonement for the sins of the people. Now Jesus is continually in God's presence, interceding on our behalf. This is the hope to which the writer refers. This also is the hope that anchors us during times of change. The emotion that comes with change can be draining, but stay the course knowing that you are anchored.

TODAY'S ASSIGNMENT

WHAT COMES TO MIND WHEN YOU THINK OF THE PURPOSE OF AN ANCHOR?

DAY 36

Isaiah 43:19

"See, I am doing a new thing! Now it springs up; do you not perceive it? I am making a way in the wilderness and streams in the wasteland."

There was a movie made about the life of Steve Jobs, Co-Founder of Apple, in 2015. The part of the movie that most resonates with me, even now, is when after he had been forced out in 1985, he returned in 1997 with some pretty wild ideas. Remember, Apple was a computer company. That is what they did. However, Jobs as CEO launched an advertising campaign called "Think Different." This was bigger than marketing; it was a thought process that swept through the company and lead to the iMac, iPod, iTunes… and the list goes on. With that, can we just agree that the greatest victories or accomplishments in our lives will come with the winds of change?

TODAY'S ASSIGNMENT

WHAT COULD YOU DO IF YOU BEGAN TO "THINK DIFFERENT?"

_____
_____
_____
_____
_____
_____
_____

DAY 37

Numbers 23:19

"God is not a man, so He does not lie. He is not human, so He does not change His mind. Has He ever spoken and failed to act? Has He ever promised and not carried it through?"

God is consistent. His promises are sure. His word is His bond. He can be counted on to be what we need Him to be when we need Him to be it.

TODAY'S ASSIGNMENT

WHAT THINGS IN YOUR LIFE DO YOU NEED TO TRULY ENTRUST TO GOD?

_____

_____

_____

_____

_____

_____

_____

DAY 38

Psalm 66:12

"You caused men to ride over our heads; We went through fire and through water; But you brought us out to a wealthy place.

Fire is used to purify metals in a process called smelting. In the same way, tests and trials in our lives serve a similar purpose. They help us see from different perspectives, and oftentimes, the truth about our character. Even in these times, God is still faithful to protect us, walk with us and give us grace and wisdom for the moment. Remember, the blessing is on the other side of through.

TODAY'S ASSIGNMENT

WHAT IS GOD SAYING TO YOU RIGHT NOW?

_____
_____
_____
_____
_____
_____
_____

DAY 39

Hebrews 12:11

"No discipline is enjoyable while it is happening-it's painful. But afterward, there will be a peaceful harvest of right living for those who are trained in this way."

I estimate this is the biggest understatement in the bible. It may just be me, but not only is discipline not enjoyable, but it can be downright painful. But it is not as painful as the consequences of wrong actions and misdirection. Correction is the foundation of change.

TODAY'S ASSIGNMENT

WHO DO YOU USE AS YOUR ACCOUNTABILITY PARTNER AND IN WHAT AREAS DO THEY HELP YOU?

_____

_____

_____

_____

_____

_____

_____

DAY 40

Proverbs 3:5-6

"Trust in the Lord with all your heart, lean not on your own understanding but in all your ways acknowledge Him and He will direct your paths."

An often overlooked step in the change process is our willingness to be directed. The bible says in Psalm 37:23 that "the Lord makes firm the steps of the one who delights in him." In other words our steps can be ordered, made sure and directed if we will just submit our hearts and ways to Him. We have all had situations where we look back and after taking an honest assessment have to admit we got ourselves into "that." If we want a different outcome then we have to take different steps. The offer still stands to have your steps made firm, are you ready?

TODAY'S ASSIGNMENT

NAME 3 THINGS THAT YOU NEED TO SEEK GOD ON?

_____
_____
_____
_____
_____
_____
_____

EMBRACE YOUR CHANGES | **REFLECTION**

What will I do today?

What was/were my goal(s) again?

What will I do this week?

What will I do next week?

What will I do this month?

"If you want to change the world, start by making your bed."

Admiral William McRaven

Congratulations,

you have made it through the first 40 days of The RESET Devotional. These next 10 days are dealing with

---

TARGETING YOUR IMPACT

is where we ask ourselves "what do I hope to accomplish by doing this?" How does our achieving this goal create an impact on the environment around us, the people in our lives, our business, our ministry, and our families, or is it just about me? The information you have in your hand is all designed to bring mindset transformation. Your "ah-ha" moment in all of this, if you haven't had it yet, no worries. This is important because it expands our "why" to a place that will keep us going when the road gets hard or when giving up seems tempting. Now is time to put a bow on your RESET.

DAY 41

Proverbs 22:1
"A good name is to be chosen rather than great riches, and favor is better than silver or gold."

Many people live in the moment and the outcomes of the moment. However, it is not until we become super clear on what we want out of life that we begin to think about the long-term impact we want to have. In other words, our legacy. To have a long-lasting impact, we must give real thought to why we do what we do. When we can get there, we can better figure out what it is that we want people to say of our contribution to the world, our families and friends.

TODAY'S ASSIGNMENT

WHAT IS THE ONE WORD THAT YOU WOULD WANT PEOPLE TO USE TO DESCRIBE THE IMPACT THAT YOU MADE ON THEM? (THIS IS YOUR LEGACY WORD!)

_____
_____
_____
_____
_____
_____

DAY 42

Philippians 3:13-14
"Brothers, I do not consider that I have made it my own. But one thing I do: forgetting what lies behind and straining forward to what lies ahead, I press on toward the goal for the prize of the upward call of God in Christ Jesus."

In this letter, Paul explains that he does not have it all figured out, but despite that, he continues to "press on toward the goal." He was saying to them that he understands that there is more to do, and though he does not know all the steps per se, he is going to keep going because the impact will be great. He knows that there is an ultimate reward for him and all those who go after the call of God in their lives. Our impact on the world is directly related to us fulfilling the call of God in our lives. In other words, we know our purpose.

TODAY'S ASSIGNMENT

WHAT DO YOU BELIEVE GOD IS SAYING TO YOU ABOUT YOUR PURPOSE?

___

___

___

___

___

___

___

DAY 43

Habakkuk 2:2-3

"And the Lord answered me: 'Write the vision; make it plain on tablets, so he may run who reads it. For still the vision awaits its appointed time; it hastens to the end—it will not lie. If it seems slow, wait for it; it will surely come; it will not delay.'"

If you study this text you will find that the Prophet Habakkuk came to God with a complaint and that God responded by telling him to get a vision. The legacy we leave will be proportionate to the vision we had. The question we must answer is this: "Are we attaching the desires of our heart to a complaint or a vision?"

TODAY'S ASSIGNMENT

COMPLAINING AND COMPLACENCY ARE TWO ENEMIES OF IMPACT. HOW ARE YOU DOING IN THESE AREAS?

_____

_____

_____

_____

_____

_____

DAY 44

2 Chronicles 15:7

"But you, take courage! Do not let your hands be weak, for your work shall be rewarded."

Azariah encouraged Judah's men to keep up the good work "for their work would be rewarded." Most interesting to me though, is when he tells them "do not let your hands be weak." Sometimes when we are working on goals that are longer term, we tend to allow ourselves to slip a little. What I mean is we stop doing the things that are necessary to maintain our strength. It is important to be dedicated to what we are doing; however, it is equally as important to ensure we do what is necessary to reenergize ourselves so that our endurance does not fail us.

TODAY'S ASSIGNMENT

HOW DO YOU REENERGIZE?

_____

_____

_____

_____

_____

_____

_____

DAY 45

Psalm 37:4
"Delight yourself in the Lord, and He will give you the desires of your heart."

There is a big difference between receiving the desires of your heart and the appetites of the flesh. Seeking God first in all we do is a sure way to be certain that what we desire lines up with God's will for our lives.

TODAY'S ASSIGNMENT

HOW CAN PURUSING AN APPETITE OF YOUR FLESH KEEP YOU FROM MAKING THE IMPACT YOU WANT TO MAKE?

_____
_____
_____
_____
_____
_____
_____

DAY 46

Mark 16:15

"And He said to them, 'Go into all the world and proclaim the gospel to the whole creation."

Jesus told the disciples to tell everyone that He had paid the penalty for sin. This single act changed humanity for all time and the disciples, simple men were charged to spread the good news. Imagine for a moment how they must have felt. How do you follow what Christ did? We can assume that some feeling said, "Man, I am not cut out for this." We probably have all been here at times in our lives where we felt like we were not "cut out for this." Be encouraged, because remember God promises never to leave us nor forsake us. The reality is… we are not cut out for this, "we were built for this!" Now go out there and make an impact!

TODAY'S ASSIGNMENT

THROUGH ACHIEVING YOUR GOAL(S), WHAT WILL BE THE IMPACT ON OTHERS?

_____
_____
_____
_____
_____
_____
_____

DAY 47

Proverbs 24:27

"Prepare your work outside; get everything ready for yourself in the field, and after that build your house."

We should carry out our work in its proper order. If a business owner invests money in a house while their business is struggling, they may lose both. Understand that it is possible to work hard and still lose it all if we do things, not in their proper timing. The impact we have depends on proper timing.

TODAY'S ASSIGNMENT

WHAT IS YOUR PERSONAL WORK SYSTEM? HOW DO YOU GO ABOUT GETTING THINGS DONE?

_____

_____

_____

_____

_____

_____

DAY 48

Luke 14:28
"For which of you, desiring to build a tower, does not first sit down and count the cost, whether he has enough to complete it?"

When the housing market crashed in 2008, I remember driving through what I thought was a neighborhood under construction, but what I found was a building project that had been abandoned. What I later found out was the builder had to stop construction because the cost had gotten too high. Now, this is an extreme example, and there were probably things that were out of their control. However, we can still see from this the importance of counting the cost. We may not be able to account for every circumstance, but we can do our due diligence. Be sure to count the cost of impact.

TODAY'S ASSIGNMENT

WHAT IS GOD SAYING TO YOU?

_____

_____

_____

_____

_____

_____

_____

_____

DAY 49

Matthew 19:26

"But Jesus looked at them and said, 'With man this is impossible, but with God all things are possible.'"

God specializes in the impossible! You may have a big vision, but you have an even bigger God.

TODAY'S ASSIGNMENT

LIST 5 WORDS THAT COME TO MIND WHEN YOU READ THIS SCRIPTURE?

_____
_____
_____
_____
_____
_____
_____

DAY 50

John 3:30
"He must increase, but I must decrease."

The greatest accomplishment that any of us can have is to help pave the way for someone else to reach their full potential. In contrast, the great failure we can have is to live a life where we do not help anyone else "get there." This scripture is John the Baptist saying that it was time for him to take a step back so that Jesus could be who God sent him to us to be. His work was not done, but in that time and space, he had prepared the way. This scripture is also the foundation of what my company, J330Life, is all about. With the opportunities you have before you, who are you going to prepare the way for?

TODAY'S ASSIGNMENT

WHO IS ON YOUR LIST?

_____

_____

_____

_____

_____

_____

_____

Self-Reflection 360

The best way to begin to define the target for your impact is to categorize your actions. As you go through the Self-Reflection 360 you will be able to see where your actions will have the most impact and be able to set a hard target for what happens when your goal is accomplished. Whether it's actions or behaviors, what could you Do More of, Do Less of, Continue to do, Start doing or Stop doing that helps set you up to have the impact you want to have?

**HOW TO ANSWER THE SELF-REFLECTION 360
(THERE ARE NO RIGHT OR WRONG ANSWERS, THIS IS YOUR PROCESS)**

DO MORE OF
I have done this, gotten good results but have not been consistent

DO LESS OF
I have done this not gotten good results and need to reevaluate

CONTINUE TO DO
Good results, it isn't broke don't fix it

START DOING
I have put this off, need to take new action

STOP DOING
This is not helping at all

USE THE TABLE ON THE NEXT PAGE TO BEGIN THE WORK.

Categorizing Your Actions

	Do More Of	Do Less Of	Continue to Do	Start Doing	Stop Doing
1					
2					
3					
4					
5					

Over the last 50 Days you have:

Renewed Your Vision (For what you want), Eliminated Your Blocks (That are keeping you from moving forward) Simplified Your Actions (Making it less complicated to get moving) Embraced Your Changes (Identified the changes you need to make and prepared to make them) Targeted Your Impact (Determined your WHY).

So now what?

As you worked your way through this devotional you may be thinking about your faith walk and where you are. That's ok! This is a part of the process. In the beginning, I told you that the first step to renewing your vision is for God to first renew your mind and purpose. So how exactly does this happen? Glad you asked. Our Heavenly Father sent his son Jesus to die for our sins. John 15:13 says "Greater love hath no man than this, that a man lay down his life for his friends." In verse 15 Jesus says that He no longer calls us servants but friends. Because we are friends of God we know we have a right to a close unbreakable relationship with him. To seal this relationship all we need to do is ask as outlined in Romans 10:9 "if you confess with your mouth the Lord Jesus and believe in your heart that God has raised Him from the dead, you will be saved." Friends, salvation is available to all who would confess and believe.

I want to offer you the opportunity to receive that salvation today or maybe you have made this confession in the past and have gotten off track.

TODAY is your opportunity to **RESET**.

PRAY THIS PRAYER WITH ME

FATHER GOD, I COME TO YOU NOW, YOU KNOW MY LIFE, YOU KNOW HOW I HAVE LIVED, I ASK YOU FATHER, TO FORGIVE ME, AND CLEANSE ME, WITH THE PRECIOUS BLOOD, OF JESUS CHRIST, I BELIEVE THAT JESUS, DIED FOR MY SINS, AND WAS RAISED FROM THE GRAVE, WITH ALL POWER, IN HIS HANDS, NOW FATHER, **TAKE MY HEART, TAKE MY LIFE, AND USE IT, FOR YOUR GLORY, FROM THIS DAY FORWARD, I BELONG TO YOU** AND I RECEIVE RENEWED VISION BY YOUR POWER, BLOCKS ARE ELIMINATED FROM MY LIFE BY YOUR LOVE, MY ACTIONS ARE SIMPLIFIED BY YOUR WISDOM, I EMBRACE MY CHANGES BY YOUR STRENGTH AND MY IMPACT IS ON TARGET BY YOUR GUIDANCE. IN YOUR SON JESUS NAME, I PRAY-

Amen

If you prayed that prayer Congratulations! I believe with you by Faith that you are saved. Now take the next step and if you are not connected to a good bible-based ministry where the Word of God is being taught and His Love is evident, make that connection. Being around believers of "like precious faith" is one of the best things we can have in our lives to inspire, empower and encourage us to keep going and keep growing.

In the coming weeks you will start to execute on work you have done throughout the devotional. James 2:17 says: "Thus also faith by itself if it does not have works, is dead." Now is the time to go and do something new. Let's crush some goals!

3 Steps to Going and Doing

FIND ADDITIONAL SCRIPTURES THAT GO WITH YOUR GOALS AND RECITE THEM EACH DAY AS YOU WORK ON THEM. Proverbs 18:21 says: "Death and Life are in the power of your tongue." The ability to give life to your dreams and goals is in your mouth!

FIND YOUR MOST SIMPLE FIRST STEP AND GO AND DO. Psalm 119:133 reads: "Direct my steps by your word And let no iniquity have dominion over me." Each day in your quiet time ask God to order your steps. This will make it much easier to identify the steps you should and should not take.

SURROUND YOURSELF WITH A SUPPORT SYSTEM. Too often we find ourselves discouraged when we are trying something new. Especially if the process is slower than we would like. Which it usually is. Proverbs 27:17 reminds us that "As iron sharpens iron, So a man sharpens the countenance of his friend." The fact of the matter is, we all go through many times of RESET in our lives. There is nothing that says that you have to take any journey in life alone. Allow grace and space for those in your circle to help inspire, empower and encourage you to get going even when it gets hard.

Now you are ready to GO AND DO!
PEACE AND BLESSINGS

Brian

Made in the USA
Columbia, SC
30 July 2021